DECEMBER 50 COLORING PAGES FOR OLDER KIDS RELAXATION

SHIH CHIEN HUA

PUBLISHED BY:
SHIH CHIEN HUA
Copyright © 2018

SEABIRD SHOP >50FOR

FB FAN PAGE

Disclaimer

The information contained in this book is for general information purposes only. The information is provided by the authors and while we endeavor to keep the information up to date and correct, we make no representations or warranties of any kind, express or implied, about the completeness, accuracy, reliability, suitability or availability with respect to the book or the information, products, services, or related graphics contained in the book for any purpose. Any reliance you place on such information is therefore strictly at your own risk.

DECEMBER 1ST

note:

_____

_____

_____

DECEMBER 2ND

note:

_____

_____

_____

DECEMBER 3RD

note:

_____

_____

_____

DECEMBER 4TH

note:

_____

_____

_____

DECEMBER 5TH

note:

_____

_____

_____

DECEMBER 6TH

note:

_____

_____

_____

DECEMBER 7TH

note:

_____

_____

_____

DECEMBER 8TH

note:

_____

_____

_____

DECEMBER 9TH

note:

_____

_____

_____

DECEMBER 10TH

note:

_____

_____

_____

DECEMBER 11TH

note:

_____

_____

_____

DECEMBER 12TH

note:

_____

_____

_____

DECEMBER 13TH

note:

_____

_____

_____

DECEMBER 14TH

note:

_____

_____

_____

DECEMBER 15TH

note:

_____

_____

_____

DECEMBER 16TH

note:

_____

_____

_____

DECEMBER 17TH

note:

_____

_____

_____

DECEMBER 18TH

note:

_____

_____

_____

DECEMBER 19TH

note:

_____

_____

_____

DECEMBER 20TH

note:

_____

_____

_____

DECEMBER 21TH

note:

_____

_____

_____

DECEMBER 22TH

note:

_____

_____

_____

DECEMBER 23TH

note:

_____

_____

_____

DECEMBER 24TH

note:

_____

_____

_____

DECEMBER 25TH

note:

_____

_____

_____

DECEMBER 26TH

note:

_____

_____

_____

DECEMBER 27TH

note:

_____

_____

_____

DECEMBER 28TH

note:

_____

_____

_____

DECEMBER 29TH

note:

_____

_____

_____

DECEMBER 30TH

note:

_____

_____

_____

DECEMBER 31TH

note:

_____

_____

_____

DECEMBER 32TH

note:

_____

_____

_____

DECEMBER 33TH

note:

_____

_____

_____

DECEMBER 34TH

note:

_____

_____

_____

DECEMBER 35TH

note:

_____

_____

_____

DECEMBER 36TH

note:

_____

_____

_____

DECEMBER 37TH

note:

_____

_____

_____

DECEMBER 38TH

note:

_____

_____

_____

DECEMBER 39TH

note:

_____

_____

_____

DECEMBER 40TH

note:

_____

_____

_____

DECEMBER 41TH

note:

_____

_____

_____

DECEMBER 42TH

note:

_____

_____

_____

DECEMBER 43TH

note:

_____

_____

_____

DECEMBER 44TH

note:

_____

_____

_____

DECEMBER 45TH

note:

_____

_____

_____

DECEMBER 46TH

note:

_____

_____

_____

DECEMBER 47TH

note:

_____

_____

_____

DECEMBER 48TH

note:

_____

_____

_____

DECEMBER 49TH

note:

_____

_____

_____

DECEMBER 50TH

note:

_____

_____

_____

www.ingramcontent.com/pod-product-compliance
Lightning Source LLC
Chambersburg PA
CBHW081605220526
45468CB00010B/2774